NEW JERSEY

in words and pictures

BY DENNIS B. FRADIN

ILLUSTRATIONS BY RICHARD WAHL

MAPS BY LEN W. MEENTS

Consultant
Dr. Donald Baird
Princeton University

CHILDRENS PRESS ™

CHICAGO

For Lawrence G. Evans

Seaside Heights, New Jersey

Library of Congress Cataloging in Publication Data
Fradin, Dennis B
  New Jersey in words & pictures.
    1. New Jersey—Juvenile literature. [1. New Jersey]
I. Wahl, Richard, 1939-1 II. Meents, Len W III. Title.
F134.3.F7   974.9   80-19688
ISBN 0-516-03930-X

Picture Acknowledgments:
NEW JERSEY DIVISION OF TRAVEL AND TOURISM, BOX 400,
TRENTON 08625—cover, 2, 13, 22, 26, 27, 28, 30, (left), 31 (right), 32,
33, 35, 36, 37, 39, 41
PRESS BUREAU, CITY OF ATLANTIC CITY—30 (right), 31 (left)
NEW JERSEY STATE LIBRARY—6, 29
LIBRARY OF CONGRESS—15
NEW JERSEY DEPARTMENT OF ENVIRONMENTAL PROTECTION,
DIVISION OF PARKS AND FORESTRY—20, 24
COVER PHOTO: New Jersey farm scene

New Jersey

New Jersey was named for Jersey, an island in the English Channel. New Jersey has big cities where many products are made. It has small farms. Forests, lakes, and the Atlantic Ocean help make it beautiful.

Much important history took place in this small state. Americans won a big Revolutionary (rev • oh • LOO • shun • airy) War battle at Trenton. Grover Cleveland was born in New Jersey. Woodrow Wilson lived there for a long time. Both became presidents.

Do you know where the first baseball game was played? Or the first college football game? Do you know where the electric light was invented? Or where a dinosaur skeleton was first found in the United States?

If you haven't guessed, the answer to all these questions is: New Jersey, the Garden State!

Between 70 and 200 million years ago, dinosaurs roamed the land. They all died out long ago. But their bones have been found. In 1858 a skeleton of the duck-billed Hadrosaurus (HAD • reh • soress) was found in New Jersey. This was the first dinosaur skeleton found in the United States.

About one million years ago the weather turned cold. The Ice Age began. Huge mountains of ice, called *glaciers* (GLAY • shurz), moved slowly down from the north. They covered northern New Jersey. The glaciers ground up rocks into soil. They spread the soil over the land. Glaciers also carved out valleys. During these cold times, mammoths and mastodons roamed the land. They looked like big, hairy elephants. All that thick hair helped keep them warm!

The Ice Age ended about 10,000 years ago. Melting glaciers filled the valleys with water. In this way many lakes were formed in northern New Jersey.

Henry Hudson's men trading with the Leni-Lenape Indians

The first people came to the area over 12,000 years ago. Their stone tools and weapons have been found. The people hunted in the forests. They fished in rivers and streams. They learned to farm. Little else is known about New Jersey's early people.

Indians in New Jersey may have been related to the ancient people. The main tribe in New Jersey called themselves the Leni-Lenape. This means "original people." Today, they are usually called the Delaware. That is because they lived near the Delaware River.

The Delaware Indians built houses out of tree bark and grass. They hunted deer and bears in the forests. The people ate the meat. They made clothes out of the skins. The Indians fished. They gathered clams in the Delaware River. They also farmed. Corn, beans, and squash were some of their crops.

The Delaware were a peaceful people. One Delaware custom was to always keep a pot of food boiling. This was in case hungry strangers came.

It is thought that Giovanni da Verrazano (jho • VAHN • nee dah vehr • reh • ZAHN • oh) was the first explorer to reach New Jersey. Verrazano was an Italian who sailed for France. He anchored near Sandy Hook in 1524.

Henry Hudson, an Englishman, arrived in 1609. Hudson
sailed for the Dutch (people of The Netherlands). In his
ship, the *Half Moon*, Hudson explored the Sandy Hook
area. The Dutch sent other explorers. They were glad
that the Indians were friendly. The Dutchmen wanted to
trade with them.

In 1618 the Dutch built a trading post at Bergen. There, they traded with the Indians for beavers and other furs. In 1660 Bergen (now Jersey City) became New Jersey's first town.

In 1664 England took control of the area. They did it without a fight. They just sailed in with some warships. Then they took the land from the Dutch. The English gave the Indians liquor, tools, and clothes. In return, Indians signed papers giving the English their lands. Some Indians fought to keep their lands. But the English had guns. Most of the Indians were pushed out.

In 1702 New Jersey became a *royal colony.* That meant it was ruled by governors from England. At this time, England ruled other colonies in America, such as New York and Connecticut. English people from these colonies came to live in New Jersey.

The settlers cut down trees and built houses. The people farmed. Like the Indians, they grew corn and beans. Wheat became a big crop.

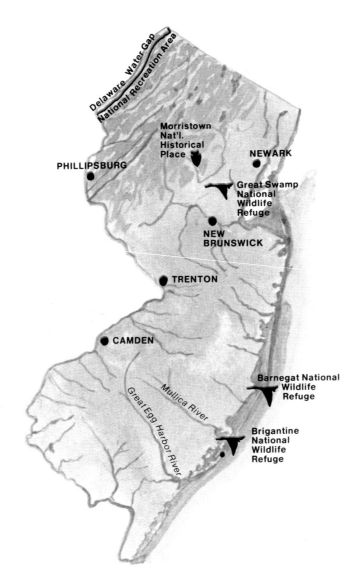

The settlers did everything for themselves. They made
bread out of their own wheat. They made soap and candles
out of animal fat. They made clothes and furniture.
Families traded with each other. One family with a cow
might trade milk for clothes. Log schools were built, too.
There, children of all ages learned together.

Where many people settled in an area, towns grew. Salem, Newark (NEW • erk), Shrewsbury (SHROOZ • burry), Elizabeth, and Trenton were some of the growing towns of the early 1700s.

Even in the 1700s, New Jersey towns were becoming manufacturing centers. That means many things were made there. Forests were cut. The wood was made into ships. Some of the ships were used in whale hunts off the New Jersey coast. Iron was made. Glass, leather, and beer were other products. Many products were sold in nearby New York City and Philadelphia (fill • ah • DELL • fia).

From 1754-1763 England fought—and won—the French and Indian War. New Jersey men helped England fight the French and the Indians. Men from the other colonies fought, too. England needed money to pay for this war. "You have to pay higher taxes!" English governors told the American colonists. Tea and other items had high taxes.

The colonists grew angry. They had built farms and towns with little help from England. They had helped England fight the French and the Indians. Now, they were told to pay big taxes.

The people were also starting to think of themselves as Americans, not English. "We'll form our own country!" people said at town meetings. "Let's unite the thirteen colonies."

You may have heard of the Boston Tea Party. That is when Americans destroyed English tea. New Jersey had its own "tea party." In 1774 some young men in Greenwich (GREN • ich) dressed up as Indians. Some tea from England was hidden in a cellar. Greenwich, New Jersey must have smelled sweet the night of December 22, 1774. That was when the men burned the English tea.

At first the colonists fought the English with words and small acts like tea burning. Then war began. This war to free the United States from England is called the Revolutionary War.

General George Washington's winter quarters were in Jockey Hollow during 1779-1780.

Thousands of New Jersey men joined George Washington's American army. New Jersey was a big Revolutionary War battleground. Nearly 100 battles were fought there.

You know that the Americans won the Revolutionary War. But for a long time it looked as though they would lose. In December of 1776 the American army was in bad shape. The English had pushed them all the way back through New Jersey into Pennsylvania. On December 25, soldiers fighting for the English were having a Christmas celebration in Trenton. They had no idea that the ragged American army would attack. An attack was just what George Washington had in mind on that freezing night.

Washington and his soldiers took boats across the Delaware River into New Jersey. Then they marched into Trenton. They opened fire. George Washington led the American army to victory in this important battle. It is known as the Battle of Trenton.

In New Jersey the Americans also won battles at Princeton, Red Bank, and Paulus Hook. The United

George Washington meeting with General Lee at Monmouth

States had won the Revolutionary War by 1783. You
probably know that Washington, D.C. is now the capital
of the United States. But for four months in 1783,
Princeton, New Jersey was the nation's capital. For about
two months in 1784 Trenton was the U.S. capital.

On December 18, 1787 New Jersey became the third state. Trenton became the state capital in 1790. Many New Jersey people had vegetable farms and gardens. New Jersey was nicknamed the *Garden State*.

A famous gun duel took place in New Jersey in 1804. It was fought between Aaron Burr and Alexander Hamilton.

Burr had been born in Newark, New Jersey. He was the vice-president of the United States.

Hamilton had helped found the city of Paterson, New Jersey. He had been the secretary of the treasury of the United States.

Burr was very angry. Hamilton had worked to keep him from becoming president. Burr challenged Hamilton to the gun duel. On the morning of July 11, 1804 they met

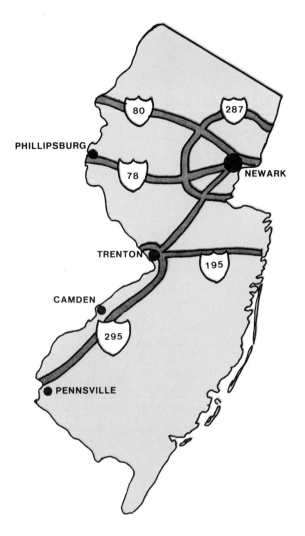

in Weehawken (we • **HAW** • ken), New Jersey. At a signal, both men fired their guns. Hamilton was killed. You can see Alexander Hamilton's picture on the $10 bill.

In the early 1800s better roads were built in New Jersey. Often, they followed old Indian trails. Roads were important to the young state. Some led to Philadelphia and New York City. There, New Jersey products and crops were sold.

In the early 1800s some New Jersey people had large farms, called *plantations*. Black slaves did the work there. Most New Jersey farmers owned no slaves. They worked their small farms themselves. In fact, many New Jersey people hated slavery. In those years, slaves who escaped to Canada were free. On the way north, slaves hid in houses of people who disliked slavery. This system of hiding slaves on the trip northward was called the "Underground Railroad." Jersey City and Perth Amboy were important stations on the Underground Railroad.

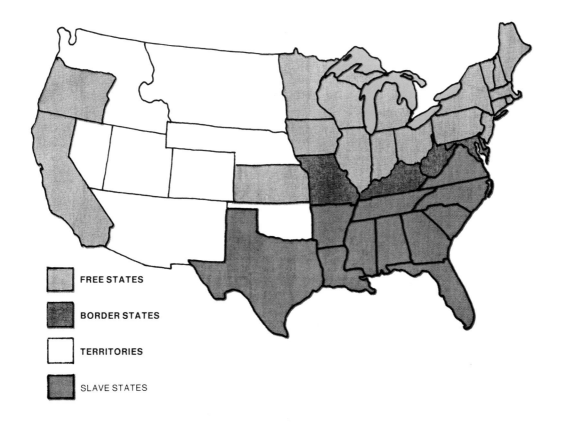

FREE STATES

BORDER STATES

TERRITORIES

SLAVE STATES

In the 1850s Americans in the North and South argued. They argued about slavery and other issues. It turned into fighting. This was the Civil War, fought from 1861 to 1865. On one side were the Northern, or Union (YOON • yun), states. On the other were the Southern, or Confederate (kon • FED • er • it), states.

New Jersey sided with the North. It sent about 88,000 men to help the Union win the Civil War.

Thomas Edison's home in Glenmont

After the Civil War, a young man named Thomas Edison moved to Menlo Park, New Jersey. He became a great inventor. Do you ever listen to a record on a record player? Edison made the first record player in 1877. In 1879 he made his most famous invention. This was the electric light. Think of "The Wizard of Menlo Park" the next time you switch on a light. Edison also improved the movie camera.

You remember how Aaron Burr had wanted to be president. Grover Cleveland, born in Caldwell in 1837, did become president. Not only that, he was president two

CLEVELAND

WILSON

separate times. He was our 22nd president from 1885 to
1889. Then a new president was elected. In 1892
Americans wanted Cleveland back. He served as the 24th
president from 1893 to 1897.

Woodrow Wilson was born in Staunton (STANT • n),
Virginia, in 1856. He moved to New Jersey. He was
elected governor. Then, in 1912, he was elected 28th
president of the United States.

The story of New Jersey in the 1900s is that of
manufacturing. Newark, Jersey City, Paterson, and other
cities turn out many products. People from around the
world have come to work in the cities.

Princeton University

New Jersey has also become a center for science
research. One reason scientists go to New Jersey is that
Princeton, Rutgers, and other fine schools are there. New
Jersey scientists have made new medicines. They have
discovered vitamins. They have built space satellites. In
1962 they made one called Telstar I. It sent TV pictures
across the Atlantic Ocean. Do you have a "transistor"
radio? It's the kind you don't have to plug in. The
transistor was first made by New Jersey scientists, too.

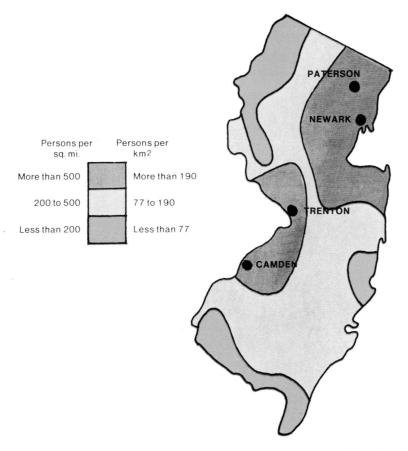

Persons per sq. mi.		Persons per km2
More than 500		More than 190
200 to 500		77 to 190
Less than 200		Less than 77

PATERSON

NEWARK

TRENTON

CAMDEN

New Jersey is one of the smallest states. Yet by 1960 it was a leading state in number of people. Some cities became too crowded. There wasn't enough good housing. In the 1960s and 1970s old buildings were torn down in Newark and other cities. New, better homes were built.

Large cities brought another problem. By the 1970s New Jersey's air and water were polluted. From an airplane, you could see a layer of smoke above much of the state. New Jersey lawmakers have worked on laws to clean up the air and water.

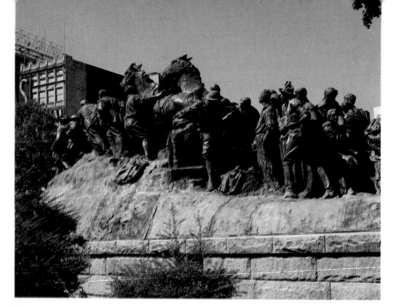
Wars of America Memorial in Newark

You have learned about some New Jersey history. Now it is time for a trip—in words and pictures—through the state.

You are in a jet high above New Jersey. Do you see that body of water stretching east as far as you can see? That is the Atlantic Ocean. New Jersey lies on the coast of the Atlantic Ocean, in the eastern United States.

Your airplane is landing in the state's biggest city. This is Newark. Like most of New Jersey's biggest cities, it is in the northeastern part of the state.

For many years, Delaware Indians lived in this area. Newark is a very old American city. It was first settled in 1666 by some families from Connecticut.

The Great Falls of the Passaic River

Today, Newark is a great manufacturing city. When you are sick, you may take medicine made in Newark. Many chemicals are made there. Clothes and food products are also made.

Some Newark products are sent just 10 miles east, to New York City. Some products go by boat from Newark Bay. They are shipped to cities around the world.

You'll see many kinds of people in Newark. There are many black people. There are people of Puerto Rican, Italian, Portuguese, Irish, Polish, and many other backgrounds.

Some products available from the Garden State

Visit the Newark Museum. There you can see art works and learn about science. The museum also has a *planetarium*. It shows planets and stars on a ceiling. Visit the New Jersey Historical Society in Newark. There you can learn about the history of the Garden State. You might also enjoy the Plume House. It was built about 1710 and is thought to be the oldest house standing in Newark.

From Newark, go about 5 miles east to Jersey City. Jersey City is even older than Newark. Dutch traders arrived in 1618. Settlers soon followed. Today, Jersey City is the state's second biggest city.

Jersey City factories turn out many products. Clothes, chemicals, and food products are just three of them.

From Liberty Park in Jersey City, New York City can be seen.

You'll enjoy seeing the Old Bergen Church in Jersey City. They don't call it old for nothing! It was built in 1660.

Jersey City has a giant clock that tells what time it is *now*. It's called the Colgate Clock. Its big hand really is big—over 2,000 pounds! People across the Hudson River in New York City can tell time by this huge clock.

Paterson is about 15 miles northwest of Jersey City. Alexander Hamilton wanted to form a city on the Passaic (peh • SAY • ik) River. He wanted it to be a place where many things were made. The town was founded on the Fourth of July in 1792. It was named after William Paterson, New Jersey governor at the time.

Above: Tom's River chemical plant
Right: The "Great Falls" in Paterson

Visit the Old Gun Mill in Paterson. Samuel Colt once made his famous guns there. Visit the Paterson Museum. There you can see a submarine. It was built by a schoolteacher named John P. Holland. Holland tested this submarine in the nearby Passaic River in 1878. It sank, and had to be pulled up from the water. Holland kept trying. In 1881, Holland built the first submarine that did work.

One of New Jersey's nicknames is the *Workshop of the Nation.* That is because so many things are made in its cities. New Jersey is the leading chemical-making state. Clothes, foods, and plastics are other main products. What do you use to call a friend? What do you sometimes watch after school? Telephones and TVs are also made here.

Northeastern New Jersey is also home to some sports teams. The Giants of the NFL play football in East Rutherford. The Nets of the NBA are New Jersey's basketball team. New Jersey has always been a big sports area. The first baseball game ever played was in Hoboken, New Jersey, in 1846. The score was 23 to 1! And the game was only four innings long. The first college football game ever played was at New Brunswick, in 1869. Rutgers beat Princeton 6 to 4 in this game.

The first college football game

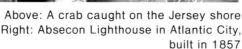

Above: A crab caught on the Jersey shore
Right: Absecon Lighthouse in Atlantic City,
built in 1857

From the big cities in the northeast, head down the
coast of the Atlantic Ocean. Once, pirates such as
Blackbeard lurked near the coast. Today, you'll see
fishing boats instead of pirate ships. Fishing is also done
in Delaware Bay and in the state's rivers. Clams, lobsters,
oysters, tuna, and flounder are seafoods brought in by
New Jersey fishermen.

Sandbars and islands off the coast make the New
Jersey shore dangerous for boats. Lighthouses were built
to guide boats to shore. Barnegat (BAR • neh • gat)
Lighthouse is pretty. Some call it "Old Barney." Sandy
Hook Lighthouse is one of the oldest in the United States.

Atlantic City (above) is a popular convention center.
Left: Many tourists visit the boardwalk in Atlantic City.

New Jersey's Atlantic shore is a big vacation area. People go there to sail or enjoy the beaches. Visit Atlantic City, in southeastern New Jersey. It has the famous "boardwalk." This is a long pathway near the ocean. Have you ever seen the Miss America Pageant? It is held in Atlantic City.

Asbury Park and Cape May are two other vacation areas. President Abraham Lincoln liked to vacation in Cape May.

About 25 miles northwest of Atlantic City, visit Batsto. This village produced cannon balls for George Washington's army. The town has been rebuilt to look as it did in Washington's time.

Batsto Village

Near Batsto there is a large forest area known as the Pine Barrens. It has pine trees and swamps. In all, about half of New Jersey is covered by forests. The wolves that once howled in the woods are gone. But you might see deer. Foxes, otters, and raccoons also live in the state. If you see a turtle looking hungrily at your hand, move it! Snapping turtles live in the swamp areas.

About 40 miles northwest of the little town of Batsto you will come to the city of Camden. It lies just across the Delaware River from Philadelphia, Pennsylvania. Camden was founded in the late 1600s by a religious group called *Quakers*.

Left: The home of William Trent who gave
Trenton its name.
Above: The State House

Visit the Walt Whitman Home in Camden. Whitman
was a famous poet. He wrote a book of poems called
Leaves of Grass. Whitman felt that he could learn a lot by
talking to people. He liked to talk to the children of
Camden. He would sometimes ride in stagecoaches just to
meet new people.

Follow the winding Delaware River about 30 miles
northeast of Camden. You'll come to the city of Trenton.
Trenton was founded in 1679 by Quaker farmers. Trenton
is the capital of New Jersey.

Visit the State Capitol building in Trenton. This is
where New Jersey lawmakers meet. You might enjoy
watching them make laws for the Garden State.

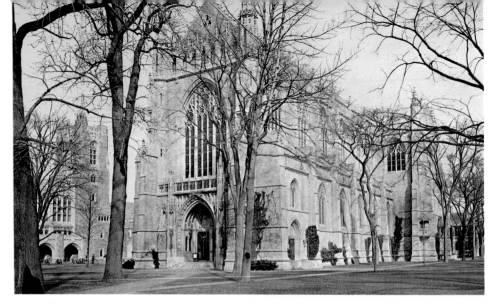

The chapel at Princeton University

Visit the William Trent house. It was built in 1719. The city of Trenton was named after Trent.

You'll also enjoy the New Jersey State Museum in Trenton. There you can learn about Indians and New Jersey history.

The city of Princeton is just a few miles northeast of Trenton. Princeton University is there. It is one of the world's most famous schools. Presidents James Madison and Woodrow Wilson studied there.

You know that you're not supposed to fight in school. But part of the Battle of Princeton was fought at Princeton University, in Nassau Hall! This was during the Revolutionary War.

A herd of beef cattle

From Princeton, head into northern New Jersey. You'll see pretty lakes. You'll see many farms. Much of New Jersey is still farmland. If you ate nothing but food from New Jersey, you'd eat well! Corn, barley, soybeans, and wheat are grown in the fine soil. Tomatoes, lettuce, and other vegetables are also grown. Apples, cranberries, and blueberries are some of the fruits. Some farmers raise milk cows. Others raise beef cattle. Chickens, turkeys, and eggs are other farm products.

Above: A New Jersey horse farm
Left: Pumpkins are grown in northern New Jersey.

Don't think farmers just plant their seeds and *hope* they'll grow. Today, farming is a science. Many farmers go to college to study about seeds, soils, and farming methods.

In farm areas, New Jersey has many small towns. Life in a small town is much different than life in the cities. There might be one bank in town and just a few stores. People know each other. You'll enjoy Cranbury, Riverdale, Chester, and other small towns. People will show you places where George Washington marched by with his soldiers. New Jersey people are proud that George Washington spent so much time there. Seven different towns are named Washington!

The Ford Mansion in Morristown

Morristown is a good place to finish your New Jersey trip. George Washington and his army spent two winters in Morristown. Visit the Ford Mansion in Morristown National Historical Park. Washington himself spent a winter there. In 1777 George Washington had the soldiers build a fort at Morristown. It was built to defend supplies. Some people thought it was built just to keep the soldiers busy. So it was named Fort Nonsense. You can see the rebuilt Fort Nonsense at the Historical Park, too.

Places can't tell the whole story of New Jersey. Many interesting people have lived in the Garden State.

James Fenimore Cooper was born in Burlington, New Jersey in 1789. One day he was reading a book out loud to his wife. He said that he could write a better book. She dared him to try. James Fenimore Cooper became a famous writer. *The Deerslayer* and *The Last of the Mohicans* are two of his books.

Mary Mapes Dodge was born in New York City in 1831. When she was a young woman, she moved to Newark. She became a writer of children's stories. She wrote the book *Hans Brinker, or, The Silver Skates.*

Joyce
Kilmer's home

Joyce Kilmer was born in New Brunswick in 1886. He was a writer, too. He wrote a famous poem called "Trees." He was killed in World War I at a very young age.

Paul Robeson was born in Princeton in 1898. He was a black man who became a famous singer and actor. He appeared in plays and films. *Show Boat* and *The Proud Valley* are two of his films.

Alice Paul was born in Moorestown, New Jersey, in 1885. When she was young, American women weren't allowed to vote in many states. Alice Paul knew this was wrong. She led marches and helped form groups. Her work helped all American women gain the right to vote in 1920. Alice Paul introduced the first Equal Rights Amendment to Congress in 1923. She is sometimes called the "mother of the Equal Rights Amendment."

Did you ever hear Frank Sinatra sing? Sinatra was born in Hoboken, New Jersey. Did you ever see a Jerry Lewis film? Lewis was born in Newark. Did you ever watch Franco Harris carry a football? Harris was born in Fort Dix, New Jersey, in 1950.

One New Jersey man really went far. Edwin Eugene Aldrin, Jr. was born in Glen Ridge, New Jersey, in 1930. He became an Air Force pilot. Later, he became an

Victorian homes in Cape May

astronaut. "Buzz" Aldrin landed on the moon in 1969. He
was the second person to walk on the moon.

Home to the Delaware Indians . . . Presidents
Cleveland and Wilson . . . and Edwin Aldrin.

A state that has farming . . . fishing . . . and big-city
factories.

The leading chemical-making state.

Scene of the first college football game and the first
baseball game.

This is New Jersey — the Garden State.

FACTS ABOUT New Jersey

Area—7,787 square miles (46th biggest state)

Greatest Distance North to South—166 miles

Greatest Distance East to West—57 miles

Highest Point—1,803 feet above sea level (High Point)

Lowest Point—Sea level (on the Atlantic Ocean)

Hottest Recorded Temperature—110° (at Runyon, on July 10, 1936)

Coldest Recorded Temperature—Minus 34° (at River Vale, on January 5, 1904)

Statehood—Our 3rd state, on December 18, 1787

Origin of Name—New Jersey was named for the island of Jersey in the English Channel

Capital—Trenton (1790)

Previous Capitals—Perth Amboy and Burlington

Counties—21

U.S. Senators—2

U.S Representatives—14

State Senators—40

State Assemblymen—80

State Motto—*Liberty and Prosperity*

Nicknames—The Garden State, the Workshop of the Nation, the Cockpit of the Revolution

State Flag—Adopted in 1896

State Seal—Adopted in 1928

State Flower—Purple violet

State Bird—Eastern goldfinch

State Animal—Horse

State Insect—Honeybee

State Tree—Red oak

State Colors—Buff and blue

Main Rivers—Delaware River and Hudson River

Some Mountain Ranges—Kittatinny, Ramapo, Watchung

Lakes—Over 800 (Lake Hopatcong is the biggest)

State Parks—40

State Forests—11

National Park—Morristown National Historical Park

State Forests—10

National Park—Morristown National Historical Park

Animals—Deer, rabbits, foxes, raccoons, skunks, minks, opossums, muskrats, woodchucks, weasels, squirrels, chipmunks, rattlesnakes and other snakes, giant sea turtles, snapping turtles, terrapins, wild turkeys, pheasants, quail, partridges, herring gulls, great blue herons, many other kinds of birds

Fishing—Clams, crabs, lobsters, flounder, tuna, scallops, oysters, porgy, menhaden, bass, pickerel, pike, sturgeon, trout

Zinc
Vegetables
Nursery Products
Dairy Products
Dairy Products
Hay
Gravel Sand
PATERSON
Beef Cattle
Nursery Products
Stone
Oats
Iron Ore
Stone
Vegetables
NEWARK
Poultry
Wheat
Vegetables
Corn
Clay
Corn
Dairy Products
Nursery Products
Wheat
Oats
Soybeans
Potatoes
TRENTON
Fruit
Vegetables
Corn
Wheat
Fruit
Poultry
Poultry
CAMDEN
Soybeans
Vegetables
Soybeans
Dairy Products
Cranberries
Sand and Gravel
Soybeans
Sand and Gravel
Vegetables
Corn
Hogs
Fruit
Fish
Sweet Potatoes
Vegetables
Fruit
Corn
Poultry
Forest Products
Clams
Stone Clay
Beans
Titanium
Berries
Grapes
Oysters
Sweet Potatoes
Magnesium

43

Farm Products—Tomatoes, lettuce, cabbage, asparagus, potatoes, beans,
   sweet corn, peaches, apples, blueberries, cranberries, strawberries, grapes,
   barley, soybeans, wheat, milk, chickens, turkeys, eggs, beef cattle
Mining—Basalt, zinc, granite, clay, limestone
Manufactured Products—Chemicals, many kinds of food products, televisions,
   radios, and other electric products, many kinds of metal products, printed
   materials, glass products, clay products, paper products, cars, clothing,
   scientific instruments
Population—7,365,011 (1980 census)

Major Cities—	Newark	329,248	(1980 census)
	Jersey City	223,532	
	Paterson	137,970	
	Elizabeth	106,201	
	Trenton	92,124	
	Camden	84,910	

New Jersey History

There were people in the New Jersey area at least 12,000 years ago.

1524—Giovanni da Verrazano, sailing for France, explores the New Jersey
   coast
1609—Henry Hudson, sailing for the Dutch, explores the coast
1618—The Dutch build a trading post at Bergen (now Jersey City)
1638—Swedish settlers arrive
1643—About 80 Delaware Indians are murdered in a raid
1660—The trading post at Bergen becomes New Jersey's first town
1664—England takes control from the Dutch
1666—Newark is settled by families from Connecticut
1676—Area is divided into East and West Jersey
1702—East and West Jersey are joined to form the English royal colony of
   New Jersey
1737—Population of New Jersey colony is about 47,000
1746—Princeton University is founded
1758—Brotherton, at Indian Mills, becomes the first Indian reservation in
   America
1763—Sandy Hook Lighthouse (now one of the oldest in America) is built
1766—Rutgers, The State University, is founded
1774—English tea is burned in the "Greenwich Tea Party"
1775—Start of Revolutionary War
1776—Americans win Battle of Trenton on December 26
1777—On January 3, Americans win Battle of Princeton; George Washington
   and U.S. troops spend the rest of the winter at Morristown
1778—Battle of Monmouth ends in a draw
1779-1780—Washington and U.S. troops spend another winter at Morristown
1783—United States has won the Revolutionary War; Princeton is the capital
   of the United States for four months

1784—Trenton is the nation's capital for two months

1787—On December 18, New Jersey becomes the 3rd state!

1790—Trenton becomes the capital of New Jersey

1792—Alexander Hamilton helps to found Paterson

1804—Alexander Hamilton is killed by Aaron Burr in a gun duel at Weehawken

1831—One of the first locomotives in America, the *John Bull,* runs on the
Camden and Amboy Railroad in New Jersey

1838—Samuel Morse, living at Morristown, demonstrates his new invention,
the telegraph

1846—World's first organized baseball game is played at Hoboken (score is
23-1 in a four-inning game!)

1858—First dinosaur skeleton ever found in the United States—a
Hadrosaurus—is discovered at Haddonfield

1861-1865—During the Civil War, New Jersey sends about 88,000 men to
fight in the Union army

1869—First college football game is played between Rutgers and Princeton

1879—Thomas Edison of Menlo Park invents the electric light

1881—John P. Holland of Paterson tests the first submarine that works

1884—Grover Cleveland, born in Caldwell, is elected the 22nd president

1887—Happy 100th birthday, state of New Jersey!

1892—Grover Cleveland is elected the 24th president; in this same year the
great poet Walt Whitman dies at Camden

1911—Woodrow Wilson becomes governor of New Jersey

1912—Wilson is elected 28th president of the United States

1914-1918—During World War I, New Jersey contributes soldiers, weapons,
and ships for the war effort

1921—The second radio station in the United States, WJZ, is founded at Newark

1932—Amelia Earhart flies from Los Angeles, California to Newark, New Jersey;
this is the first nonstop airplane flight across the country by a woman

1939-1945—During World War II, over 560,000 New Jersey men and women
are in uniform

1947—Transistor is invented by three New Jersey scientists

1952—New Jersey Turnpike is finished

1962—Telstar I, a satellite designed in New Jersey, is sent into orbit

1967—Race riots in Newark result in 26 deaths

1969—State lottery is approved to raise money for the state; in this same year
Edwin Aldrin becomes the second person to walk on the moon

1976—State income tax is begun

1980—As severe drought conditions continue, compulsory water rationing for
114 communities in northern New Jersey is imposed by Governor Byrne

1984—Record rains fall, causing rivers to overflow in 6 counties in
northern New Jersey. More than 6,000 people evacuate their homes

1985—The New York Jets football team moves home to the Giants Stadium in
the Meadowlands; Garden State Race Track at Cherry Hill is rebuilt after
shut-down by fire

45

INDEX

INDEX, Cont'd

About the Author:

Dennis Fradin attended Northwestern University on a creative writing scholarship and graduated in 1967. While still at Northwestern, he published his first stories in *Ingenue* magazine and also won a prize in *Seventeen's* short story competition. A prolific writer, Dennis Fradin has been regularly publishing stories in such diverse places as *The Saturday Evening Post, Scholastic, National Humane Review, Midwest,* and *The Teaching Paper.* He has also scripted several educational films. Since 1970 he has taught second grade reading in a Chicago school—a rewarding job, which, the author says, "provides a captive audience on whom I test my children's stories." Married and the father of three children, Dennis Fradin spends his free time with his family or playing a myriad of sports and games with his childhood chums.

About the Artists:

Len Meents studied painting and drawing at Southern Illinois University and after graduation in 1969 he moved to Chicago. Mr. Meents works full time as a painter and illustrator. He and his wife and child currently make their home in LaGrange, Illinois.

Richard Wahl, graduate of the Art Center College of Design in Los Angeles, has illustrated a number of magazine articles and booklets. He is a skilled artist and photographer who advocates realistic interpretations of his subjects. He lives with his wife and two sons in Libertyville, Illinois.